KUWAIT

...in Pictures

Courtesy of F. Mattioli/FAO

Visual Geography Series®

KUWAIT

...in Pictures

Prepared by
Geography Department

Lerner Publications Company
Minneapolis

Independent Picture Service

Rapid evaporation of water causes a jigsaw pattern to form in the parched desert soil of Kuwait.

This is an all-new edition of the Visual Geography Series. Previous editions have been published by Sterling Publishing Company, New York City, and some of the original textual information has been retained. New photographs, maps, charts, captions, and updated information have been added. The text has been entirely reset in 10/12 Century Textbook.

LIBRARY OF CONGRESS CATALOGING-IN-PUBLICATION DATA

Kuwait in pictures / prepared by Geography Department, Lerner Publications Company.

    p. cm. — (Visual geography series)
    Rev. ed. of: Kuwait in pictures / prepared by Camille Mirepoix.
    Includes index.
    Summary: Photographs and text introduce the geography, history, government, people, culture, and economy of the small oil-rich country on the Persian Gulf.
    ISBN 0-8225-1846-5
    1. Kuwait. [1. Kuwait.] I. Mirepoix, Camille. Kuwait in pictures. II. Lerner Publications Company. Geography Dept. III. Series: Visual geography series (Minneapolis, Minn.)
DS 247.K8K77 1989
953'.6705—dc19
                           88-9445
                           CIP
                           AC

International Standard Book Number: 0-8225-1846-5
Library of Congress Catalog Card Number: 88-9445

VISUAL GEOGRAPHY SERIES®

Publisher
Harry Jonas Lerner
Associate Publisher
Nancy M. Campbell
Senior Editor
Mary M. Rodgers
Editor
Gretchen Bratvold
Assistant Editors
Dan Filbin
Kathleen S. Heidel
Illustrations Editor
Karen A. Sirvaitis
Consultants/Contributors
Dr. Ruth F. Hale
Isaac Eshel
Sandra K. Davis
Designer
Jim Simondet
Cartographer
Carol F. Barrett
Indexer
Sylvia Timian
Production Manager
Richard J. Hannah

Independent Picture Service

A crew of foreigners and Kuwaitis works on an oil-drilling rig at Burgan oil field.

Acknowledgments

Title page photo courtesy of Kuwait Ministry of Information, Safat.

Elevation contours adapted from *The Times Atlas of the World*, seventh comprehensive edition (New York: Times Books, 1985).

1 2 3 4 5 6 7 8 9 10 98 97 96 95 94 93 92 91 90 89

Beginning in the 1950s, city planners used the profits from oil to construct shaded parks in Al-Kuwait, the nation's capital.

Contents

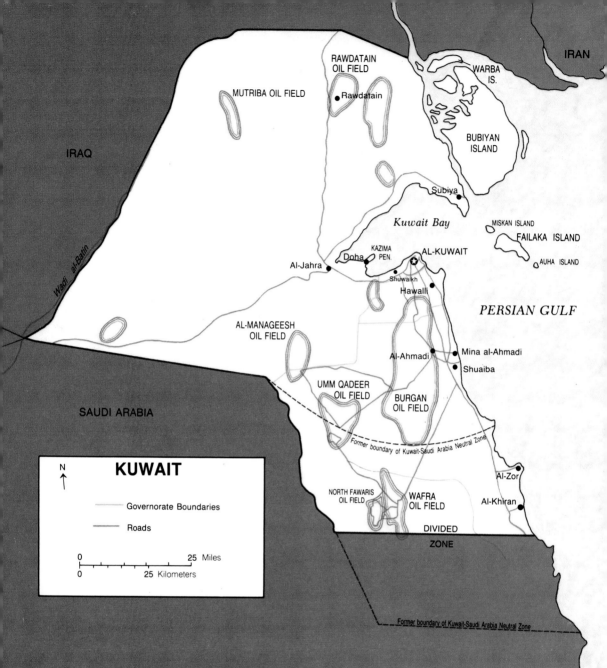

IRAN

RAWDATAIN
OIL FIELD

WARBA
IS.

MUTRIBA OIL FIELD

● Rawdatain

BUBIYAN
ISLAND

IRAQ

Subiya ●

Kuwait Bay

MISKAN ISLAND

FAILAKA ISLAND

KAZIMA
PEN.

AL-KUWAIT

AUHA ISLAND

Doha ●

Al-Jahra ●

Shuwaikh

Hawalli

PERSIAN GULF

AL-MANAGEESH
OIL FIELD

Al-Ahmadi ●

● Mina al-Ahmadi

● Shuaiba

UMM QADEER
OIL FIELD

BURGAN
OIL FIELD

SAUDI ARABIA

Former boundary of Kuwait-Saudi Arabia Neutral Zone

Al-Zor ●

N

KUWAIT

NORTH FAWARIS
OIL FIELD

WAFRA
OIL FIELD

Al-Khiran ●

——— Governorate Boundaries

——— Roads

DIVIDED

ZONE

0   25 Miles

0   25 Kilometers

Former boundary of Kuwait-Saudi Arabia Neutral Zone

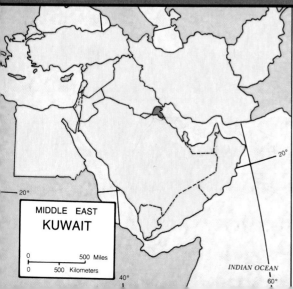

20°

20°

MIDDLE EAST
KUWAIT

0   500 Miles

0   500 Kilometers

INDIAN OCEAN

40°

60°

Seif Palace, the administrative headquarters of Kuwait's ruling family, commands a front position along the coast in Al-Kuwait.

Introduction

Surrounded by desert sands, the Middle Eastern country of Kuwait sits on one of the world's largest proven reserves of oil. As a result of this vast source of income, Kuwait has embarked on a new era of progress since the mid-twentieth century. Since the discovery of oil in 1938 Kuwait has moved away from a past marked by poverty, lack of water, and desert heat. Until that time Kuwait had served primarily as a stopping point along sea and caravan routes to more important trading centers. Commerce, boat building, and diving for pearls in the Persian Gulf had been the main sources of income for Kuwait.

Ahmad al-Jabir al-Ahmad al-Sabah, who ruled Kuwait from 1921 to 1950, oversaw much of the nation's transformation into a wealthy state. By granting exploration rights to the British- and U.S.-owned Kuwait Oil Company in 1934, he laid the foundation for the nation's oil industry. The venture was so successful that an oil trade arose, bringing in earnings that funded the construction of the port of Al-Ahmadi in the 1940s.

In 1950 Abdallah al-Salim al-Sabah inherited control of Kuwait and poured the profits from oil into additional improvements for the country. The effort created

Huge tankers berth at a pier in Mina al-Ahmadi, the largest port for Kuwait's oil industry.

employment for every Kuwaiti and many more jobs for foreign workers. Schools, hospitals, houses, parks, gardens, and modern government buildings multiplied. The Sabah ruling family and creative administrators developed plans for the present and the future.

In many areas, expanses of stone and steel replaced the sands of the desert. Trees that thrive in warm, dry places were planted along the city streets, and flowerbeds began to bloom. Local industry, suqs (outdoor markets), shops, and supermarkets opened for business. In the once sleepy fishing village of Al-Kuwait, the capital city, the development since the mid-twentieth century has been extensive.

As a member of OPEC (the Organization of Petroleum Exporting Countries) and as the owner of one of the world's largest oil companies, Kuwait plays a prominent role in regional and international affairs. Although Kuwait has used profits from oil to buy regional security, it was unable to avoid conflict during the 1980s with Iran, which lies across the Persian Gulf. The issue of regional security, coupled with tension between the nation's Sunni and Shiite populations—who represent the two major sects of the Islamic religion—makes Kuwait's future uncertain.

A spacious pathway leads to Al-Hilaly Mosque, one of hundreds of Islamic places of worship in Kuwait. Muslims, or followers of Islam, make up 85 percent of the nation's population.

Dusk falls on a harbor in Kuwait Bay, where traditional Arab boats, or dhows, line the shore. Throughout Kuwaiti history, people living in the region have turned to the sea for their livelihoods.

1) The Land

Forming a wedge of territory between Iraq and Saudi Arabia, Kuwait lies in the desert on the northwestern coast of the Persian Gulf. Iraq borders the country to the north and west, and Saudi Arabia forms Kuwait's southern and southwestern boundaries. A section of territory—known as the Divided Zone—in the southeast is split between Saudi Arabia and Kuwait. Each country governs its own portion, but they share the oil resources in this region equally.

With an area of about 6,800 square miles, Kuwait is slightly smaller than the state of New Jersey. This area includes several islands, of which Failaka is the most populated. Among the others are Bubiyan, Warba, Miskan, and Auha. Although Bubiyan is the largest island, it is uninhabited because it is low-lying and marshy.

Topography

The main topographic feature of Kuwait is the indentation in the coastline that forms Kuwait Bay. The sheltered waters of this inlet enable the capital city of Al-Kuwait and other points along the shore to maintain a position of maritime importance in the busy Persian Gulf.

About 25 miles south of the capital is the town of Al-Ahmadi, located on a 400-foot-high ridge. This uplift and two others in the north interrupt the flatness of the desert. These high points are very important because they enable crude oil to flow by gravity from nearby oil fields to the

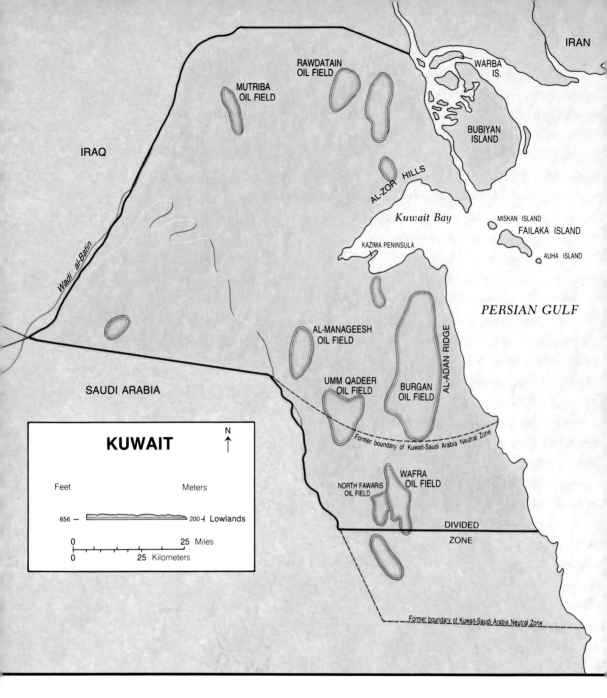

coast. From there the oil is easy to export.

Lack of rain is evident everywhere in Kuwait. A small oasis (fertile area) at Al-Jahra breaks the monotony of the desert. Only wind—which creates interesting rock formations—shapes and weathers the low-lying desert. A few marshes and lagoons line Kuwait Bay, but no major mountains, no rivers or streams, and very little natural vegetation add variation to the desert landscape.

Water Resources

With no permanent fresh water supply, the country relies primarily on huge desalinization plants, which remove salt from sea water. Several shallow wadis, or dry streambeds that fill with rain only during

Although most of Kuwait is flat terrain, rocky cliffs—such as the Al-Zor Hills—occasionally break the uniformity of the desert.

the short winter, converge at Rawdatain. Here, pure, mineral-rich rainwater collects in the wadis before evaporating or sinking into the dry soil. This water, along with brackish (salty) reserves at several other places, supplements the water resources. Brackish water is used for irrigating crops, for cleaning streets, and for watering herds

Water desalinization plants generate electricity as well as purify water. This power station at Shuaiba uses the distillation method to extract salt from sea water.

11

of livestock. Distilled (purified) water is sometimes mixed with brackish water to decrease the strength of the salt.

The giant turbines of distillation plants —in which sea water is first steamed, leaving the salts behind, and is then recondensed in huge vats—also produce enough electrical power to meet the needs of Kuwait's industry. In 1984 the Doha Reverse Osmosis Plant opened. The plant uses reverse osmosis—a process that draws the salt out of the water—instead of the energy-demanding distillation method to create fresh water from sea water.

Climate

With a typically semitropical desert climate, Kuwait has extremely hot summers and cool winters. Summer temperatures may exceed 120° F, and in August and September the humidity increases, making the heat more uncomfortable. Sandstorms often occur between May and July.

From November to April the climate is mild, with a pleasant coolness in the evenings. In January, the coldest month, temperatures average between 50° and 60° F. In the interior of Kuwait, frost sometimes occurs, but the temperature along the coast, which is moderated by the gulf waters, remains warmer.

Most of Kuwait's rain falls in the winter between October and April. Although precipitation levels are unpredictable, the country averages only from one to seven inches of rain each year. In a good year, enough rain falls to turn the desert green in March and April.

Flora and Fauna

During the winter, when a little rain falls, sheep and goats graze on desert flowers and grasses that cover the wadis. The most common desert shrub is the *arfaj*, which may reach two and a half feet in height. Nomadic herders around Wadi al-Batin in the west use arfaj for firewood. Although forests do not exist naturally in Kuwait, trees have been planted in residential areas to provide relief from the scorching desert sun.

Gazelles, foxes, and jackals once roamed Kuwait but are no longer found. Birds—including swallows, wagtails, chiffchaffs,

A date grower climbs to the top of a palm tree to gather the ripened fruit. Harvests from a single tree can reach 600 pounds per year.

The hulls of dhows frame fishing boats in the Persian Gulf.

skylarks, and wrens—migrate from other regions throughout the year. Some Kuwaitis keep hawks, which they train to use in hunting. Kuwaiti herders raise camels, goats, and sheep for meat and milk. Fish caught in the Persian Gulf supplement the diets of both people and animals in Kuwait.

Al-Kuwait

The capital of the State of Kuwait, Al-Kuwait is a modern metropolis built by the oil-rich government as a showpiece of modern architecture. With about 89,000 people (excluding suburbs) the city thrives as an administrative, commercial, and financial center. Modern hotels and high-rise office buildings stand alongside the tall minarets (towers) of mosques (Islamic houses of worship). Al-Kuwait's banking facilities are among the largest in the Middle East.

The winding streets, marketplaces, and mud-brick structures that once characterized Al-Kuwait have been torn up and replaced with modern roads and buildings funded by the oil industry. Many of the capital's residents are foreigners who have come to fill jobs created by the country's rapid industrialization. The outskirts of Al-Kuwait have also grown in recent years, and many surrounding communities have evolved. Hawalli, the largest suburb, has more people than the capital itself does.

Some Kuwaitis still practice the ancient art of falconry, or hunting with trained hawks. The traditional sport is commemorated on the nation's coat of arms by a falcon (hawk) with outspread wings.

Profits from the oil industry have been used to rebuild Al-Kuwait, turning the nation's capital into a modern city that makes use of many technological advances.

The homes of wealthy merchants in Al-Kuwait are spacious and luxurious.

14

The town of Al-Ahmadi houses many employees of Kuwait's oil industry.

Although most urban women in Kuwait wear Western clothing, conservative women dress according to tradition.

15

Secondary Communities

Greenery, pleasant gardens, and villas that are set along tree-lined avenues grace the town of Al-Ahmadi. Nearby is the port, Mina al-Ahmadi. The city has about 27,000 people and is the center for the nation's oil production. Situated in the middle of Burgan oil field, the town sits on Al-Adan ridge, which rises 400 feet above sea level. Al-Ahmadi lies about 25 miles south of Al-Kuwait, to which it is connected by expressway.

Al-Jahra (population 11,000) is one of Kuwait's oldest communities. Indeed, evidence suggests that it flourished before Islamic armies conquered the area in the seventh century A.D. Long an agricultural town, Al-Jahra is now urbanized, and modern buildings have replaced most of the old farms.

Failaka Island lies 20 miles east of the mainland opposite Kuwait Bay and is approximately 8 miles long. In the 1960s archaeological excavations revealed traces of an ancient settlement on Failaka, and scientists concluded that Greek ships had used the island as a stopover base. Extensive ruins of a city suggest that there was once an established population, but what

happened to these original inhabitants is a mystery. Today both foreign and Kuwaiti tourists vacation along Failaka's sunny beaches. The people on the island make a living as farmers, teachers, and resort workers, or they commute to work in Al-Kuwait each day by ferryboat.

Two new towns, Subiya in the north and Al-Khiran in the south, are being developed to accommodate the country's rapidly expanding population. The first phase of construction is focusing on Al-Khiran because it is close to major centers of industry. Once an uninhabited desert area south of Al-Kuwait, Al-Khiran now is a modern tourist resort with restaurants, cafeterias, and playgrounds, as well as swimming pools, tennis courts, a sailing marina, and a ship repair yard. Urban planners expect the population of Al-Khiran to reach 115,000 by the year 2005.

Subiya will house more than 250,000 people. New schools, gardens, a 500-bed hospital, and several clinics are planned. Work on a new road leading to Subiya has been completed. A bridge links the settlement to Bubiyan Island, where development plans include recreational facilities, research centers, and fish-canning plants.

Located a few miles down Kuwait Bay southwest from the capital, the port at Shuwaikh is equipped with cranes for loading and unloading cargo.

With their huge eyes showing awed adoration of the gods and their hands clasping cups used in religious ceremonies, these figurines are the work of early Sumerians and date from about 2500 B.C. Thought by some historians to be an extension of Al-Ubaid culture from the area of Kuwait, the Sumerian civilization arose in the Euphrates River Valley just north of Kuwait. Cuneiform, the wedge-shaped writing developed by these people, was used throughout the Middle East for about 2,000 years.

2) History and Government

Lying in the northeastern corner of the Arabian Peninsula, Kuwait shares much of its history with other areas of the peninsula. Indeed, its present-day boundaries did not become fixed until the twentieth century. The growth of Islam—a religion established in the seventh century A.D. by the prophet Muhammad—was the dominant force in Arabian history. Historians know little about the region before the Islamic conquest.

Early Civilizations

Despite the lack of written records, archaeologists have discovered evidence of human

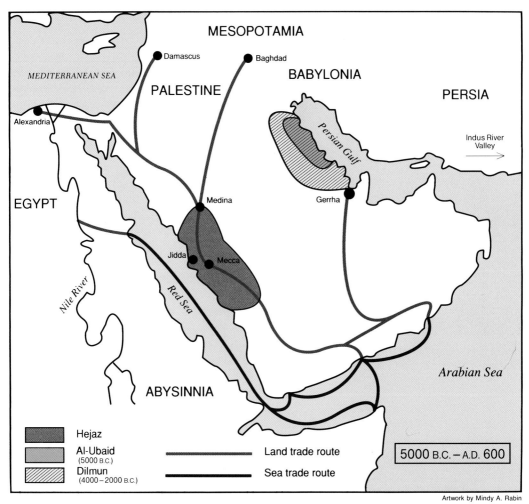

MESOPOTAMIA

BABYLONIA

PERSIA

PALESTINE

MEDITERRANEAN SEA

● Damascus ● Baghdad

Persian Gulf

Indus River
Valley

Alexandria

EGYPT

Medina

Gerrha

Jidda ● Mecca

Nile River

Red Sea

Arabian Sea

ABYSINNIA

	Hejaz
	Al-Ubaid (5000 B.C.)
	Dilmun (4000–2000 B.C.)

—————— Land trade route

—————— Sea trade route

5000 B.C. – A.D. 600

Artwork by Mindy A. Rabin

Throughout recorded history, trade routes have crossed the Arabian Peninsula, linking the region with peoples to the west, north, and east. About 5,000 years ago, the Dilmun civilization (the northern section of which was located in present-day Kuwait) traded with inhabitants of the Indus River Valley to the east. In later centuries, peoples from this area of the peninsula exchanged goods with Arabs to the north, south, and west.

existence in the area of Kuwait as far back as 5000 B.C. Part of the Al-Ubaid culture, the people from this period are identical to the first people known to have settled and cultivated Mesopotamia (modern Iraq) to the north.

Archaeologists have yet to determine whether the ancient Al-Ubaid culture began in northern Arabia along the northwestern coast of the Persian Gulf or in Mesopotamia. If Arabia was the birthplace of the Al-Ubaid culture, then these Arabian people were ancestors of the Sumerians from southern Mesopotamia—

the first people in the world known to have developed a high culture.

DILMUN

From about 4000 to 2000 B.C. the Dilmun civilization extended along the coast from present-day Kuwait to the island of Bahrain in the south. A people who made their living from seafaring raids, the residents of Dilmun controlled the route to India at their peak in 2000 B.C., carrying goods between Mesopotamia and the Indus River Valley in present-day Pakistan. The Mesopotamians regarded the city-state of

Ancient stone tablets have been found on land near the western shores of the Persian Gulf. The 2,000-year-old artifacts are engraved in an ancient script from southern Arabia.

Dilmun as a holy place whose people were blessed.

Dilmun's commercial power began to decline around 1800 B.C., perhaps because the Indus Valley was invaded at that time and the culture there was destroyed, thus ending trade with the region. Piracy flourished throughout the Persian Gulf during Dilmun's decline. Although Dilmun continued to trade, kingdoms in southern Arabia gained commercial control of the gulf. After about 600 B.C. the Babylonians, and later the Persians, added Dilmun to their empire.

GREEK INFLUENCE

After Alexander the Great of Greece conquered Mesopotamia in the 330s B.C., Greeks established a colony on the island of Failaka. They named the island Ikaros after a Greek isle in the Aegean Sea. The site probably began as a camp for Alexander's soldiers, and gradually the colony

Courtesy of Kuwait Ministry of Information, Safat

Archaeologists have unearthed the remains of Greek buildings on Failaka Island. They have also discovered evidence of a Dilmun settlement at the southern end of the island.

became more diverse. A settlement started on the shore, where the Greeks built a temple to Artemis, goddess of the moon and the hunt. Because the island had military and strategic value, the colony expanded inland, where the Greeks constructed a fortress.

The Greek presence lasted for about 200 years, after which Greek control in the region declined. Eventually, the Romans entered the land around the Persian Gulf. After the Roman Empire made Christianity legal in A.D. 313, this new, monotheistic (one-god) religion influenced the inhabitants of the region. From this period until the rise of Islam in the seventh century A.D., little is known about the area of present-day Kuwait.

The Muslim Conquest

In about A.D. 570 Muhammad—the founder of Islam—was born at Mecca, a city in present-day Saudi Arabia. Muhammad began preaching a monotheistic religion

After succeeding his father as head of the Greek city-state of Macedon in 336 B.C., Alexander the Great extended his realm throughout Asia Minor (modern Turkey), Mesopotamia, and Persia (modern Iran).

Several hundred stone seals found on Failaka date from the early Bronze Age (2500 B.C.). Although the meaning of the symbols on these stamps remains a mystery, similar findings in Iraq, Bahrain, and the Indus River Valley support the theory that ancient Arabians traded with peoples from the Indus Valley.

20

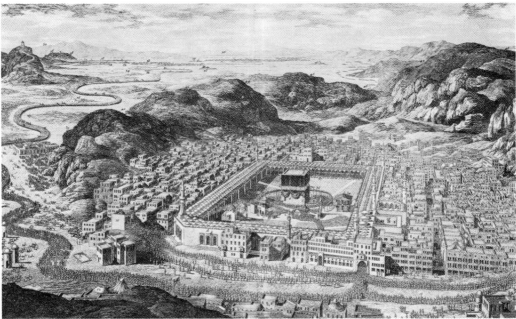

An engraving shows Al-Haram, the most sacred mosque in Mecca, and thousands of Muslims from all over the Islamic world making the hajj, or pilgrimage to the holy city in Saudi Arabia. The black-curtained building in the courtyard of the mosque is the Kaaba, believed to have been built by the prophet Abraham, from whom Muslims claim descent.

called Islam, which means "submission to the will of God." Eventually Muhammad gained many followers—called Muslims—who formed armies to extend the new faith throughout Arabia and to unify Arab peoples. By the middle of the seventh century the area of modern Kuwait was under Muslim rule.

During the early Islamic period, the main Kuwaiti settlement was on Kazima, a small peninsula in Kuwait Bay near the present town of Al-Jahra. Because it was on the bay and had relatively fertile surroundings, Kazima became a famous trading station. Muslim pilgrims paused at the site to rest from their travels, and caravans stopped on their way to Mecca and other Arabian towns. During the seventh century Muslim armies were stationed at Kazima because it was valued as a strategic point.

Indeed, in the Zat al-Salassel, or Battle of the Chains, Arab armies led by Khalid ibn al-Walid defeated the Persians at Ka-zima in about 636. The event was so named because the Persian general bound his soldiers together in a chain to prevent anyone from fleeing during battle, which enabled the Arabs to kill every soldier.

Although many details about Kuwait are unknown between the early Islamic period and the eighteenth century, the safe harbor of Kuwait Bay probably continued to attract inhabitants to the region. With only dates, pearls, and camels making up the primary resources of the area, the people turned to seafaring activities—like generations before them had—to earn a living. Lying at the center of a trade network, the Persian Gulf became an important commercial region, and maritime city-states developed and competed for control of the gulf.

A golden age of gulf shipping began in the eighth century, when Muslim leaders (called caliphs) moved the political capital of Islam from Mecca to Baghdad, Iraq. Baghdad's location north of the gulf made

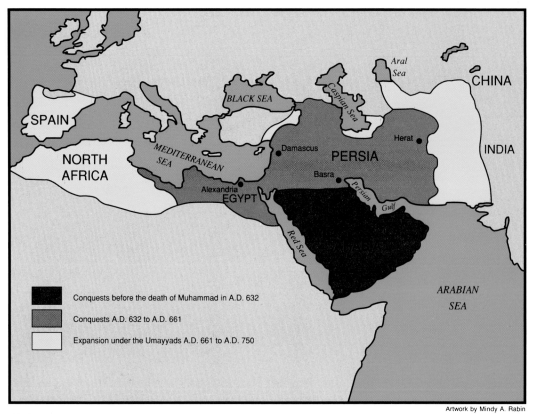

After conquering present-day Kuwait in the mid-seventh century, Muslim armies set up a base in the area, from which they attacked the Persian Empire (modern Iran). The Muslim realm eventually stretched from Western Europe to India.

the waterway a favored trade route to the capital. In the sixteenth century Portuguese, Dutch, and British powers, seeking wealth and new markets, entered the competition for control of the gulf.

The Founding of Kuwait

Kuwaiti historical records from the eighteenth century tell of a drought that struck the Arabian Peninsula in 1722. Consequently, a famine began in the central Nejd region of present-day Saudi Arabia, forcing many Arab groups—including the Utub, a subgroup of the Anaiza tribe—to migrate northeast to the Persian Gulf in search of better pasture for their herds.

At Kuwait Bay the Utub settled at a small town they called Kuwait, a form of the Arabic word *kut*, which means a fortress built near water. Although the area offered poor farming conditions and no nearby source of drinking water, it had a milder climate and was less crowded than other regions of the Arabian Peninsula.

The Utub mingled with the small population that was already in Kuwait and participated in the trading activity on the gulf. Although these people led a fairly isolated existence, when German explorer Carsten Niebuhr visited Arabia in the 1760s, he described Kuwait as having about 10,000 people and a fleet of 800 vessels. Most of the people made their living by trading, fishing, or pearling.

At least 10 extended families made up the Utub population. The Sabah family controlled the city of Kuwait, and in 1756 Sabah bin Jabir was elected to be the first sheikh (leader) of the Utub people. Descendants of the Sabah family have ruled Kuwait ever since.

Development of Trade

The Kuwaiti-based Sabah family held a particularly choice position for trade because land and sea routes connected Kuwait to commercial centers throughout the Middle East. Caravans from Aleppo, Syria, stopped in Kuwait regularly, increasing the wealth of the Sabah family and thereby enabling them to build a strong fleet of ships. Furthermore, because the Utub had strong trade relations with foreign powers, especially the British, Kuwaiti merchants did not have to become pirates in order to survive. The location of Utub merchants in a sparsely populated area gave them free access to both land and sea trade.

In 1762 Abdallah al-Sabah, son of Sabah bin Jabir, became Kuwait's second ruler. Abdallah, who ruled until his death in 1812, established patterns for future social and political development that lasted through the mid-twentieth century.

Abdallah continued the friendly relationship with the British that his father had begun. In 1775 this friendship prompted the British to move the starting point for

A verse from an illuminated Koran (the book of Islamic sacred writings) dates from the sixteenth century. The Koran explicitly forbids the depiction of human beings or any other living forms.

For several centuries the dhow, a sailing vessel used throughout Arabian waterways, represented the mainstay of Kuwait's economic activities.

its desert mail service—which ran between the Persian Gulf and Aleppo—from Persian-occupied Basra, Iraq, to Al-Kuwait. About the same time, to avoid the Persians, the British East India Company also moved its trading post from Basra to Al-Kuwait. With the British presence in Kuwait established, British forces helped to defend the Kuwaitis against attacks from the Wahhabis of Saudi Arabia at the end of the eighteenth century.

Kuwaiti merchant power became so strong in the eighteenth and early nineteenth centuries that neither the Ottoman Turks, whose empire extended to present-day Kuwait, nor the Persians across the

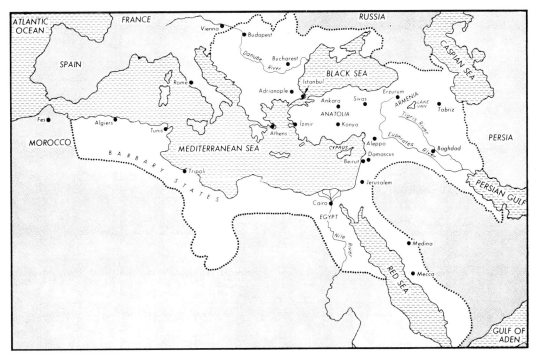

By the middle of the seventeenth century, the Ottoman Empire included all of the Middle East, much of the North African coast, and most of Eastern Europe. Map taken from *The Area Handbook for the Republic of Turkey,* 1973.

gulf were able to challenge Kuwaiti control of the major trade routes. In the late nineteenth century, however, Kuwait's sheikh Abdallah al-Sabah, who ruled from 1866 to 1892, recognized Turkish control of the region. He acknowledged their power by paying Ottoman taxes and by accepting the title of qaimaqam (commandant) of the local Ottoman administration in Basra. Ottoman rulers in faraway Turkey, however, had little involvement in Kuwaiti affairs.

A military parade shows the excellent training that made Ottoman troops hard to defeat in battle.

The British Protectorate

By the turn of the twentieth century, Sheikh Mubarak al-Sabah, who ruled from 1896 to 1915, feared that the Turks might decide to occupy Kuwait. In 1899 he signed an agreement with the British accepting their protection and acknowledging their control over Kuwait's foreign affairs. In exchange, Mubarak pledged that he and his successors would neither give up territory nor meet with officials from foreign countries without British consent. Thus began Kuwait's new status as a protectorate of Great Britain.

With British interests in the region now formally secured, the British agreed to grant the Sabah family an annual payment. Although Great Britain recognized Kuwaiti self-rule in 1914, the state remained a British protectorate until 1961. Both countries upheld treaty relations until this date, when Kuwait officially gained its independence.

The boundaries of present-day Kuwait began to take shape in the years following World War I (1914–1918). After attacks once again from the Wahhabis, who were trying to extend their realm, Kuwait reached a border agreement with Saudi Arabia in the Treaty of Uqair in 1922. At the same time, the two countries established the Neutral Zone—an area of about 2,000 square miles along Kuwait's southern limit—and they agreed to share the natural resources and the administration of this area equally. (In 1969 the two countries decided to split the Neutral Zone—since known as the Divided Zone. Each country now administers its own portion but still shares the resources.)

Although Kuwait has never formally ratified its northern border with Iraq, the line dates from an agreement made between Kuwait and the Ottoman Empire in 1913. Iraqis accepted this previously established line when their country gained independence from Turkey in 1932. Kuwait and Iraq have generally enjoyed friendly relations, but Iraq made claims to Kuwaiti territory in the 1960s and again

Courtesy of Kuwait Ministry of Information, Safat

Only the five entrances to Al-Kuwait – including Jahra Gate *(above)* **– remain of the last mud-brick wall built around the capital. Constructed in 1911, the wall was torn down in 1957 to accommodate the city's expansion. Two other fortifications – dating from 1760 and 1811 – had previously been torn down as Al-Kuwait grew beyond its original city limits.**

After the discovery of petroleum in Kuwait in 1938, a huge oil industry arose that has since funded the nation's development. At the refinery in Shuaiba, large reservoirs store petroleum products waiting to be exported.

in the 1970s. The two countries have yet to officially settle these disputes.

The Discovery of Oil

While Kuwait and its neighbors were drawing their boundaries, British Petroleum, a British oil company, requested rights to a portion of Kuwaiti territory to test-drill for petroleum. Seepages in the desert had indicated that oil lay beneath the surface, but only drilling could determine the quantity and quality of the deposits.

Gulf Oil Corporation of the United States was also interested in resources in the gulf region, and in 1932 Gulf Oil and British Petroleum formed a joint venture called the Kuwait Oil Company. In 1934 Sheikh Ahmad al-Jabir al-Ahmad al-Sabah granted Kuwait Oil permission to explore for oil.

Four years later drillers discovered oil under the desert at Burgan—now one of the largest and most productive oil fields in the world. Although exploration stopped during World War II (1939–1945), drillers found additional deposits after the war at Wafra, North Fawaris, Umm Qadeer, Al-Manageesh, Mutriba, and Rawdatain, as well as at offshore sites. Kuwaitis installed pipelines and other facilities, and commercial export began in 1946. Control of these operations, however, remained in the hands of foreign companies, despite efforts by Kuwaiti leaders to take part in policy and management decisions.

Under the provisions of a 1951 agreement, the Kuwaiti ruler shared equally in the profits of the Kuwait Oil Company. This arrangement gave Sheikh Abdallah al-Salim al-Sabah (who ruled from 1950 to 1965) the income to initiate educational and public works programs. Oil profits transformed Kuwait from an underdeveloped nation into a well-directed and well-equipped country with an extensive system of public services.

Independence

On June 19, 1961, Kuwait ended the agreement it had made with Britain in 1899 for protection, thereby achieving full independence. Sheikh Abdallah added the title of emir (ruler) to his name, and Kuwait joined the Arab League—an organization formed by the leaders of Arab states to strengthen Arab ties and to address Arab concerns. On November 11, 1962, Emir Sheikh Abdallah approved a Kuwaiti constitution written by a constitutional assembly.

During the 1960s Kuwait became increasingly wealthy as the nation's output of petroleum rose. Government policies sought to equalize the distribution of income and land among Kuwaiti citizens through welfare programs. Along with steady domestic improvements, however, the country faced regional disruptions. After Kuwait declared its independence,

Independent Picture Service

A crew from the Getty Oil Company—which jointly manages the port at Al-Zor with the Kuwait Oil Company—works in the Divided Zone.

Iraq claimed part of the new nation's territory. In the 1980s Kuwait bought border security from Iraq by financially supporting the nation in its war against Iran.

Courtesy of Kuwait Ministry of Information, Safat

A Kuwaiti official hands Sheikh Abdallah a draft of the constitution shortly after the nation gained independence.

Kuwait has also been an active supporter of the Arab cause against Israel, a nation on the eastern shores of the Mediterranean that was formed in 1948 to create a homeland for the Jewish people. Kuwait has supplied financial assistance to Arab countries that border Israel, as well as to organizations formed by the Palestinians, an Arab people who claim the land now governed by the Israelis.

After the outbreak of an Arab-Israeli war in 1973, Kuwait and other Arab oil-producing countries cut back shipments of oil to Western countries that supported Israel. Called an embargo, the halt of shipments—as well as a 70 percent increase in prices imposed by OPEC—affected consumers throughout the West.

The 1980s

A war between Iran and Iraq that erupted in 1980 threatened the production and transport of oil in Kuwait, complicating its foreign policies in the Arab world. Although Kuwait declared neutrality in this war, it supplied Iraq with financial aid and allowed foreign vessels carrying arms for Iraq to unload in Al-Kuwait.

Kuwait's relations with Iran are tense. Iran bombed Kuwaiti oil installations in 1981, and Islamic Jihad—a militant group of Shiite Muslims with connections to Iran—claimed responsibility for bombings in 1983. Kuwaitis blamed Iran for attacks on Kuwaiti shipping in the Persian Gulf in 1984. The reports of bombings hurt Kuwait's international trade and has made foreign companies hesitant to invest in the country.

Furthermore, because a large Shiite minority lives in Kuwait, the nation's leaders fear that Iran, which experienced a Shiite revolution in 1979, may sponsor Shiite coup attempts in Kuwait. In 1985 an attempt to assassinate Emir Sheikh Jabir

Independent Picture Service

Surrounded by gardens and bordered by the sea, Al-Salim Palace in Al-Kuwait is used for official receptions. The open-worked design of the V-shaped panels allows air currents to cool the outside galleries. Inside, the building is air-conditioned.

Escorted by U.S. Navy ships, Kuwaiti tankers bearing U.S. flags move through the Persian Gulf. In 1987 the United States agreed to protect all reflagged vessels from hostile attacks until they reached open waters. The cease-fire settlement agreed upon by Iran and Iraq in mid-1988 could reduce the need for U.S. fleets in the gulf.

failed. Many Kuwaitis believed that the attack was carried out by the pro-Iranian organization Islamic Voice. Following further bombing attacks, Kuwait's legislature voted unanimously to give terrorists the death penalty when their acts result in the loss of lives. In 1985 and 1986 Kuwait advised almost 27,000 foreigners living in the country—many of whom were Iranians—to leave. In the spring of 1988 a group of pro-Iranians hijacked a Kuwait Airways plane.

In late 1987, in response to Iranian bombing attacks on oil tankers, Kuwait asked the United States to escort Kuwaiti ships through the Strait of Hormuz at the entrance to the Persian Gulf. At first the United States refused, but when the Soviet Union offered to protect the ships instead, the United States felt compelled to prevent the Soviets from becoming established in the gulf. The United States agreed to escort Kuwaiti ships bearing U.S. flags, which could be obtained by registering the ships in the United States.

This protection enabled Kuwait to continue its vital international trade.

Government

Kuwait is an independent state that operates under a hereditary monarchy—that is, the ruler appoints a relative to serve as prime minister and to succeed the monarch to the throne. The constitution guarantees equal opportunities, individual freedom, and freedoms of religion and the press. It also protects the freedom to form societies and trade unions. Government powers are separated into three branches —executive, legislative, and judicial.

The head of state is the emir, who governs through a cabinet of ministers headed by the prime minister. The prime minister and other cabinet members are jointly responsible to the emir for matters concerning general policy.

Twice—from 1963 to 1976 and from 1981 to 1986—the nation's rulers have experimented with an elected legislative

Courtesy of Kuwait Ministry of Information, Safat

Unanimously approved by the National Assembly as crown prince of Kuwait, Sheikh Jabir al-Ahmad al-Sabah became emir on December 31, 1977. He is the thirteenth emir from the Sabah family, which has ruled Kuwait since 1756.

Courtesy of Kuwait Ministry of Information, Safat

The Amiri Guard band performs at an official event.

Courtesy of Kuwait Ministry of Information, Safat

Artwork by Jim Simondet

Adopted after independence in 1961, the flag of Kuwait *(left)* features the colors of the Arab world. Green stands for the earth, white for the country's achievements, red for the future, and black for the battlefields. The national coat of arms *(above)* has a falcon embracing the flag and a dhow sailing on white and blue waves—a symbol of Kuwait's maritime tradition.

body, the 50-member National Assembly. Both times, however, the emir dissolved it when representatives opposed official policies too strongly.

In 1959 Kuwaiti officials reorganized the judicial system—which is based on Islamic law, or sharia—by establishing courts of law and by adopting modern legal codes. Two kinds of courts exist in Kuwait. Courts of first instance decide personal, civil, commercial, and criminal cases. Courts of appeal rehear cases from the lower courts. Appeals from this secondary level go to the supreme court, which also rules on the constitutionality of laws. The emir acts as the final source of judicial appeal, and he is empowered to pardon those who have been convicted.

Courtesy of Kuwait Ministry of Information, Safat

A modern, technological society, Kuwait arms its military forces with sophisticated, Soviet-built equipment such as surface-to-air missiles.

Six modern stadiums—each seating 25,000 spectators—attest to Kuwaiti enthusiasm for sporting events.

3) The People

About 40 percent—or 760,000—of the 1.9 million people living in Kuwait are Kuwaiti citizens. The remaining 60 percent are non-Kuwaitis who have come to the country to reap the benefits of the oil industry. Kuwait's economic growth depends on these foreigners, who supplement the nation's work force with their expertise in science, technology, medicine, engineering, and other skills necessary to produce oil and its by-products.

In the mid-1980s the government began to encourage Iranians and non-Kuwaiti Arabs to leave the country in order to better maintain the nation's internal security. With the outbreak of the Iran-Iraq war in 1980, Kuwaiti fears have deepened over the presence of Iranians, who make up about 7 percent of the population. Furthermore, some authorities estimate that Palestinians represent at least 20 percent of Kuwait's population. In addition, 4 percent are Egyptian; 15 percent are other Arabs, who come mostly from Iraq; 7 percent are Indians; and 6 percent are Pakistanis.

The large percentage of Palestinians poses a threat to Kuwaiti stability. Many of these foreigners are educated, are politically aware, have lived in Kuwait for several decades, and some hold high positions in the government and in other fields. Consequently, Kuwaiti citizens fear that Palestinians could come to control the government and economy. Palestinians have begun to resent the legal discrimination they face in Kuwait. Foreigners lack the political and some of the social rights of Kuwaiti citizens, and officials are seeking to further restrain the power of non-Kuwaitis by increasing the ratio of Kuwaitis to 50 percent of the population.

Social Structure

As an Arab country, Kuwait traditionally has ordered its society according to a family-based rather than an economic class structure. Despite Kuwait's long-standing system of organization, however, social change has made its mark on the country. Widespread economic growth has made traditional social relationships less important, because money can buy necessities and conveniences that in the past could only be acquired through family connections. Furthermore, the growth of the capital city has reinforced the nation's urban character, which began with the arrival of the Utub in the eighteenth century. Few Kuwaitis still lead the nomadic desert lifestyle of their Arab ancestors. Indeed, 80 percent of the population lives in cities.

Independent Picture Service

Kuwaitis have given up the lifestyle of their Bedouin ancestors—nomadic Arabs who moved with their herds and lived in tents made of goatskin. The government's policy of offering employment to all citizens has encouraged the few remaining Bedouin to lead a more settled existence in the cities.

KUWAITIS

Kuwaiti citizens are a privileged and affluent class who reap the benefits of one of the best-developed welfare states in the world. Indeed, according to World Bank estimates, the nation's per capita income

Courtesy of Embassy of Kuwait

The rapid development of Kuwait's oil industry has sped up the nation's urbanization. By 1987, 80 percent of the population lived in cities.

Built by the government for low-income Kuwaiti citizens, these simple but comfortable homes each feature a courtyard. Privacy is an important element of Islamic life.

of $16,720 in 1984 tops that of many Western countries. Status among Kuwaitis is determined by religious affiliation, by ethnic background, and by the date they or their ancestors immigrated to Kuwait. Despite these levels of prestige, however, Kuwaiti citizens rarely question their position in society, since the state meets most personal needs.

Nevertheless, a class structure is beginning to take shape alongside the age-old family system of social organization.

Students from a secondary school conduct experiments in a marine biology class. Kuwaitis and foreigners alike receive state-funded education from the primary grades through the university level.

The oil refinery at Mina al-Ahmadi and other oil facilities throughout the country employ foreigners as well as Kuwaitis. Sixty percent of the nation's residents are non-Kuwaitis who help to fill the work force.

Kuwaitis are taking advantage of the opportunities of free education, which places professional jobs within the reach of all citizens, thereby increasing social mobility. Through education, many ambitious Kuwaitis from modest backgrounds have achieved great prosperity. Although family connections have long played an important role in an individual's opportunities, personal ability now also shapes a person's future.

FOREIGNERS

Since the mid-twentieth century, Kuwait's social structure has been divided into citizens and foreigners. As a result, Kuwaitis have reserved many of the best jobs for themselves, freeing up unskilled

At a Kuwaiti school festival, children from around the world hold signs that state the name of their homeland. Non-Kuwaitis living in the country represent 120 different nations.

A Danish architect designed the building for Kuwait's National Assembly in the form of an Arab tent. During periods when the legislature has been in operation, it has provided Kuwaiti citizens with a political voice.

positions for noncitizens. Some foreigners fill skilled positions when there are no Kuwaitis with the proper training, but the differences between these two groups are very clearly maintained. They generally live in separate areas, and foreigners have no political or voting rights.

Furthermore, noncitizens are restricted in the ownership of businesses and property and receive lower wages than Kuwaitis do for equivalent work. Along with Kuwaiti citizens, foreigners receive free education and health care, but they are excluded from other welfare programs, such as housing allowances and pensions (savings plans to support workers after they retire). Despite these differences, many foreigners would rather live in Kuwait than in their native countries because they can earn more money in the oil-rich nation.

Political Participation

Kuwaitis have no organized form of political participation, such as political parties or trade unions. Nevertheless, their political system has some democratic features. During periods when the National Assembly has been in session, elected representatives to this legislative body have increased the influence of lower economic groups. Kuwaiti citizens have conveyed their interests to National Assembly representatives or to members of the ruling family. Such communication is often done indirectly, through a relative or a friend who knows someone that can influence political decisions.

Decision makers can also be reached directly at a *diwaniya,* or private club for men. Such groups have historically performed a vital function in societies like Kuwait's. Diwaniyas provide a framework for solving disputes and for reaching a consensus, or group agreement, on various matters of mutual concern. As Kuwait became more urbanized in the mid-twentieth century, these clubs began to reflect a class system, with men of similar levels of wealth (and sometimes age) belonging to the same group.

Nevertheless, diwaniyas retain some of their former functions. Members sit on the floor in a loose circle, drink tea and coffee, and talk. Some subjects, such as women, are taboo; others, such as politics, may be discussed in a specific manner. In this way connections are made, and favors may be asked indirectly and discreetly through a friend. Members arrange appointments, settle contracts, make introductions, and offer jobs—all in subtle ways. As a result, each member benefits from his involvement in the diwaniya.

Male and female members of Kuwaiti families traditionally entertain at home in separate rooms. Coffee and tea are an integral part of Arab hospitality.

Family Life

The unifying factor in Kuwaiti society is the family, which Kuwaitis hold in higher esteem than they do the individual, the community, or the state. As in other Arab cultures, the traditional family unit is extended and includes a husband, his parents if they are still living, his wife, his sons and their wives and children, and his unmarried sons and daughters. Not until the father dies do his sons split away from this unit and head their own extended households with their descendants.

Traditionally, parents arrange marriages, which take place within the extended family. Unions between a father's daughter and his brother's son (who are first cousins) are considered ideal. In this way the daughter will already know the family she will be living with, and the bride-price can be lower because the marriage is contained within the family unit.

With the industrialization of Kuwait, nomadic herders, or Bedouin, have given up their wandering lifestyle in favor of the steady, paid employment offered in Kuwait's cities. These changes have decreased the size of families living together because of the limited space in urban areas. Yet the extended family remains the organizing principle in Kuwait. Even households made up of only parents and their children tend to live near relatives.

Women

Although women in Kuwait exercise more independence than women in most Arab countries, traditional values still limit their freedom, especially when compared to Western lifestyles. No longer confined to the home, women may attend school and seek employment, but they often are segregated from men in these activities.

Education, in particular, has presented Kuwaiti women with options besides those of wife and mother, and equal numbers of girls and boys entered primary schools in the mid-1980s. Although the number of women in the work force has increased steadily since the 1960s, a high percentage of female workers come from other na-tions. In 1985 over 43 percent of the non-Kuwaiti women living in the country worked, whereas less than 14 percent of Kuwaiti women were employed outside their homes. These figures suggest that Kuwaiti women have not changed their lifestyle as much as foreign women living in Kuwait have.

A man roasts coffee beans in a brass pot *(right)*, stirring them constantly so they will brown evenly. Afterward, he grinds them into a fine powder *(below)* using a mortar and pestle. Sometimes spices such as cardamom seeds are added to the coffee.

Independent Picture Service

Independent Picture Service

Independent Picture Service

Getting married and bearing children—especially males—increases a woman's standing in traditional Kuwaiti society. By the age of 20, 29 percent of the women in Kuwait have already taken husbands.

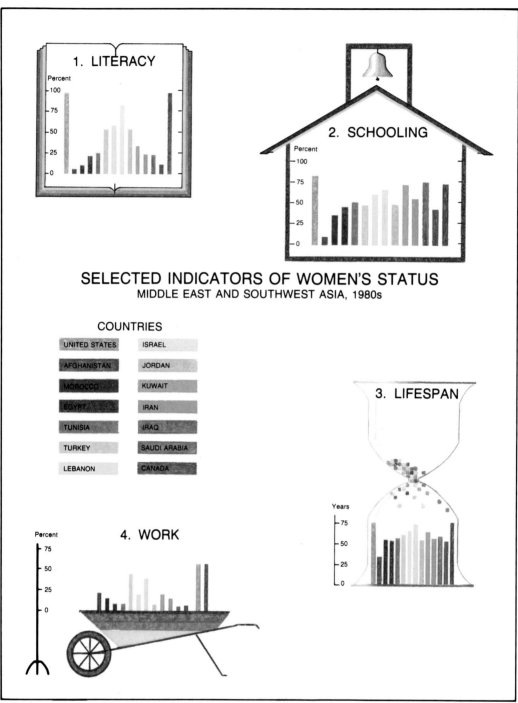

SELECTED INDICATORS OF WOMEN'S STATUS
MIDDLE EAST AND SOUTHWEST ASIA, 1980s

1. LITERACY

Percent

2. SCHOOLING

Percent

COUNTRIES

UNITED STATES	ISRAEL
AFGHANISTAN	JORDAN
MOROCCO	KUWAIT
EGYPT	IRAN
TUNISIA	IRAQ
TURKEY	SAUDI ARABIA
LEBANON	CANADA

3. LIFESPAN

Years

4. WORK

Percent

Artwork by Carol F. Barrett

Depicted in this chart are factors relating to the status of women in the Middle East and southwest Asia. Graph 1, labeled Literacy, shows the percentage of adult women who can read and write. Graph 2 illustrates the proportion of school-aged girls who actually attend elementary and secondary schools. Graph 3 depicts the life expectancy of female babies at birth. Graph 4 shows the percentage of women in the income-producing work force. Data taken from *Women in the World: An International Atlas,* 1986 and from *Women . . . A World Survey,* 1985.

Lavishly adorned with gold ornaments, this woman is ready for a festive occasion. Jewelry traditionally is a measure of an Arab woman's wealth.

Courtesy of Kuwait Ministry of Information, Safat

Attitudes toward women have begun to change in Kuwait, but traditional institutions often continue to operate as they have for centuries. For example, parents usually decide whom their children will marry. Young adults who voice their own opinion in this matter, however, are no longer forbidden to marry the person of their choice. But, because women have few contacts with men who are not family members, matches made by parents often seem suitable.

Although women traditionally have not had a direct political voice in Kuwaiti society, they have frequently influenced the decisions of male members of their family. Women began to organize formally in the 1960s when they established the Women's Social and Cultural Association. But the activities of women have been

Photo by John Grooters/Reformed Church in America

Many of the mosques in Kuwait are recently built, modern structures.

confined largely to social welfare and humanitarian programs.

In addition, Kuwaiti women have not yet gained the right to vote. Efforts in the 1980s to secure the vote for women faced strong public opposition from conservative religious groups, despite the fact that both the emir and the crown prince of Kuwait supported the movement.

Religion

Kuwaiti citizens and a large percentage of foreigners from other Arab countries practice the Islamic religion. Non-Kuwaitis from other faiths, however, include Christian groups such as Protestants and Roman Catholics.

Devout Muslims follow Muhammad's teachings, which he set forth in the Koran. Islam means "submission," and submission to the will of God, or Allah, is the guiding principle of Islam. Muslims adhere to several pillars, or duties of their faith. These include praying five times a day, fasting from sunrise to sunset during the holy month of Ramadan, and making the pilgrimage to Mecca at least once in a lifetime.

The Muslim population in Kuwait is estimated to be over 80 percent Sunni and 15 to 20 percent Shiite. The two groups represent the two major Islamic sects, which arose after the death of Muhammad in the seventh century. At that time, Sunnis agreed to elect religious leaders, whereas Shiites maintained that only descendants of Muhammad held the right to lead the Islamic community.

Most of the Shiites in Kuwait originally came from Iran, where Shiites make up a majority of the population. Some of the Shiites living in Kuwait arrived before the 1920s and thus qualified for Kuwaiti citizenship. When Shiites gained power following the 1979 revolution in Iran, they began to encourage aggressive, anti-Sunni sentiments among Shiites in Kuwait. Consequently, Sunnis in Kuwait have feared that the Shiites might disrupt Kuwaiti society. Nevertheless, the nation has remained stable, perhaps because it provides a comfortable existence to Shiite citizens and donates funding to Shiite cultural organizations.

During the 1980s another religious force arose among Kuwait's Sunni fundamentalists (conservatives). They believe that

A teacher leads a group of young children in Islamic prayer, an obligation met by faithful Muslims five times a day.

Muslims who have made the hajj, or pilgrimage to Mecca, pray under the graceful arches of Al-Haram, the holy city's greatest mosque. Constructed in the eighth century, the building has undergone frequent enlargement.

the rapid industrialization of the nation has eroded its Islamic morals. Of the many Islamic cultural organizations in Kuwait, the most influential are the Social Reform Society—which gained some seats in the National Assembly in the mid-1980s—and the Society for the Revival of Islamic Heritage. The most extreme of Kuwait's Sunni fundamentalist groups, this latter organization rejects all forms of modernization

43

Many Kuwaitis live in comfortable, middle-class homes. With government programs to fund health care and housing, the nation's citizens enjoy a high standard of living.

Photo by Robert Azzi/Woodfin Camp and Associates

and proposes that Islamic society return to the way it was during the life of Muhammad.

Health Care

The rapid increase of income from the oil industry has enabled Kuwait to greatly improve its health services since the 1950s. An infant mortality rate that stood at over 120 deaths for every 1,000 live births in the early twentieth century dropped to only 19 deaths per 1,000 by 1987. Life expectancy likewise improved dramatically. In 1987 Kuwaitis could expect to live to 72 years of age, a figure that is closer to the U.S. average of 75 than to the western Asian average of 62.

Improved health services have eliminated many threats—such as smallpox—that previously plagued the country. The main causes of death now are ailments that are common to many industrialized nations—such as heart disease, infectious and parasitic diseases, cancer, and traffic accidents.

Kuwait is divided into six health administration districts, each of which serves about one-sixth of the population. Medical facilities in each health district include a public hospital, a health center, and general and specialized clinics. By building

Courtesy of Kuwait Ministry of Information, Safat

Huge reservoirs store water that has been processed at the nation's desalinization plants. Whereas in 1950 water came by dhow and donkey from Iraq, in the late twentieth century most Kuwaiti homes received piped-in water. The greatly increased availability of fresh water has helped to improve health conditions in Kuwait.

these facilities in different areas of the country rather than only in the capital city, the Kuwaiti government has brought health care within easy reach of the entire population.

All residents—Kuwaitis and foreigners alike—receive free medical care, which is funded completely by the state. Although Kuwait still relies on a large percentage of foreign doctors, the government recently built a training hospital to increase the number of physicians who are Kuwaiti citizens. About one-third of the nation's Kuwaiti doctors are women.

In addition to its health-care system, Kuwait also provides citizens with a wide range of welfare programs. The system makes payments to the disabled, the elderly, families of students, widows, unmarried women over the age of 18, orphans, the poor, and families of prisoners.

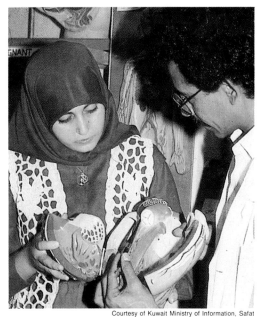

Courtesy of Kuwait Ministry of Information, Safat

A medical student examines an artificial heart under the supervision of her professor. More and more Kuwaiti women are becoming doctors.

Education

In a society that is able to provide many social services to its residents, Kuwait has made education one of its biggest concerns. The government channels large sums of money to schools, making the Kuwaiti educational system one of the best in the Middle East.

Some private schools exist in Kuwait, but they are attended mostly by foreigners, who often cannot gain admission to state-run institutions. Public schools are free from kindergarten through the university level, and education is compulsory for all children aged 6 to 14. Instructors in state-run schools teach in Arabic, the official language of Kuwait, and students aged 10 and older learn English as a second language.

Students make use of the library facilities at Kuwait University.

Courtesy of Kuwait Ministry of Information, Safat

Opened in 1966, the Kuwait University campus features modern architecture. Over half of the students enrolled at the university are female, and women account for well over half of the institution's graduates.

Courtesy of Kuwait Ministry of Information, Safat

The government covers the cost of books, uniforms, meals, and transportation, in addition to paying parents an allowance to help cover educational expenses. The state also offers scholarships to university students who study abroad. Kuwait University, which opened in 1966, has nine departments, as well as the University College for Women and the College of Graduate Studies.

In keeping with Muslim codes of modesty for women, girls attend separate schools, where they receive training in home economics, maternity, and child care. They may also prepare for jobs—as secretaries, receptionists, and teachers, for example—that are traditionally accepted for women. Although women are not encouraged to enroll in mechanical or engineering programs or to study abroad, they are gaining acceptance as medical doctors.

Educational policy since the 1960s has focused on increasing the country's literacy rate and on providing classes for adults who received little or no education when they were children. A law enacted in 1981 requires everyone who cannot read and write to enroll in classes at centers established to wipe out illiteracy.

The efforts to spread literacy are proving successful—in 1957 less than 45 per-

In 1981 the government passed a law requiring all adults who could not read and write to enroll in literacy courses. As in other Kuwaiti schools, men and women attend separate classes. The woman on the right still follows traditional Muslim codes of modesty, covering herself from head to foot. Many Kuwaiti women, however, wear Western-style clothing.

Courtesy of Kuwait Ministry of Information, Safat

cent of the population could read, whereas in the 1980s over 70 percent were literate. The literacy rate, however, still remains significantly lower among women—about 59 percent. Furthermore, foreigners, who represent the most educated segment of the population, boost the statistics. Nevertheless, the fact that 87 percent of children from 10 to 14 years of age can read holds promise for Kuwait's future development.

The Arts

The National Council for Culture, Arts, and Letters has supported the arts and has encouraged Kuwaiti writers and artists since its founding in 1974. The council spreads awareness of the arts, maintains the country's Islamic heritage, and strengthens Arab and other international ties through cultural exchanges. It sponsors an annual competition of children's paintings, for example, to foster the artistic development of young people around the world.

Painting and sculpture as forms of artistic expression have only recently been developed in Kuwait, perhaps in part because Islam forbids representations of human images. Indeed, schools did not begin to offer art classes until the mid-twentieth century. One artist who has gained prominence is the sculptor Sami Mohammed. His statue in Al-Kuwait's Safat Square is a tribute to the nation's seafaring past. It is constructed in the shape of a huge open oyster with a pearl inside the shell.

Bedouin art represents Kuwait's best-known folk art. Some Kuwaitis have recently revived Bedouin weaving, which is made from brightly colored wool on a loom called a *sadu*. The Bedouin tradition also includes dances, such as the *ardah*. Drums and tambourines accompany ardah dancers, who use swords to demonstrate their agility and bravery.

In addition to this traditional dance, many folklore troupes perform popular dances, some of which have become a part of family gatherings, social meetings,

New school curricula include art classes, which students begin at an early age in Kuwait.

Surrounded by colorful Arab weavings, musicians perform on traditional instruments.

Selected from among 140,000 entries, this painting by a Kuwaiti child received a certificate of merit at the 1983 International Children's Arts Exhibition.

Wool for *sadu,* a traditional form of Arab weaving, comes from sheep and camels and is dyed bright colors.

The Kuwait Museum houses a wide range of collections in the fields of art, history, and natural science.

and weddings. Music is also a popular art form, and the sea chantey is one of the most distinctive of Kuwaiti songs. The words, rhythms, and dances of sea chanteys traditionally accompanied various tasks performed on pearling ships.

Sports and Recreation

Soccer is the most popular sport in Kuwait, and it is played at schools and sports clubs throughout the country. The National Soccer Team has won both Arab and international competitions. Kuwaitis have also gained international recognition in horse racing.

Kuwait's location on the Persian Gulf offers great opportunities for sea sports. Clubs around Al-Kuwait provide equipment for wind surfing, water skiing, scuba diving, and yachting. Although Kuwait has many excellent beaches, people usually swim in pools because jellyfish in the gulf waters are a major hazard during much of the year. The government owns and runs several sports clubs, which have facilities for swimming, tennis, and other activities.

Young men line up for a bicycle race.

Kuwaiti youths parade at an international athletic competition.

Numerous sea clubs for water sports enthusiasts line the shores near the capital.

Situated in an excellent harbor, the port facilities of Al-Kuwait contribute to the nation's economic prosperity.

4) The Economy

Kuwait plays a role in the world's economy that is far greater than that of most countries with a similar size and population. This small, arid country ranks as one of the primary producers of oil in the world. Its proven reserves of crude oil are estimated at over 10 percent of the total world reserves. Oil accounts for 65 percent of government revenues and for 87 percent of the nation's profits from exports.

Kuwait's per capita gross national product, or GNP (the amount of goods and services produced per year), is among the world's highest—an achievement made possible by careful planning. In 1952 the government formed the Development Board to plan every aspect of Kuwait's social and

economic activity. This committee gave priority to the development of electricity and water resources because they were crucial to the progress of other plans.

A power plant at Shuwaikh, which began operating in 1954, has multiplied its capacity nearly sevenfold. A water distillation plant that had an output of 1 million gallons per day in 1953 reached 52 million gallons per day in 1973. By the 1980s its daily output had exceeded 235 million gallons. These resources aid the development of industry. In addition, Kuwait's growing population sped up construction, as new roads were built and the number of housing units was increased to accommodate more people.

The oil refinery at Shuaiba is completely powered by hydrogen and produces more than 30 types of oil. The plant's complicated, flexible control system enables production to be switched from heavy petroleum products to medium or light products at the push of a button.

The Oil Industry

The Kuwaiti government controls all aspects of its oil industry, from production to transportation and marketing. This arrangement has not always existed in Kuwait. Originally, British Petroleum of Great Britain and Gulf Oil of the United States jointly owned the Kuwait Oil Company. In 1974 the Kuwaiti government bought 60 percent of the company, and in 1976 it purchased the remainder. The government's principal aim is to use its earnings from oil to develop a wide variety of business interests. Kuwait hopes to break its dependence on oil for income, because the price and demand for oil are unpredictable.

STRUCTURE OF THE OIL INDUSTRY

The Kuwait Petroleum Corporation (KPC) plays a key role in managing the entire oil sector, and the minister of oil and industry chairs its board of directors. Since it began in 1980, KPC has reorganized the structure of the nation's oil

Valves connected to this wellhead—a device used to tap oil—control the flow of petroleum that comes up the shaft from deep under the desert.

business. The corporation gave Kuwait Oil Company responsibility for exploration, drilling, and processing of oil in all areas of the nation. Other organizations took over secondary tasks. Kuwait National Petroleum Company controls refining, local marketing, and converting gas into liquid fuel. Kuwait Oil Tanker Company organizes the transport of crude oil, liquid gas, and oil products to Kuwait's world markets.

In 1982 KPC purchased the U.S.-based Santa Fe International Corporation. In so doing, KPC joined the ranks of the seven major international oil companies, known as the "seven sisters."

OIL ACTIVITIES

Exploration activities continue both on land and under the ocean. Experts predict that known reserves will last another 250 years at late-1980s rates of production. In addition to oil, Kuwait has huge reserves of natural gas. So far, this additional resource has been used principally to maintain pressure in the oil fields, to generate

Independent Picture Service
A drilling crew extracts petroleum at Burgan, Kuwait's largest oil field.

electricity, and to produce petrochemicals and fertilizers. A liquefied gas plant at Al-Ahmadi treats and distributes gas to local users.

Independent Picture Service
An Arab-style, geometric pattern decorates the Kuwait National Petroleum Company building.

Crude and processed petroleum is stored at ports along the coast *(above),* where it is easily accessible for shipment. Smokestacks at the Petrochemical Industries plant *(right)* feature special equipment to prevent environmental pollution. A giant oil tanker berth *(below)* is part of the man-made island at Mina al-Ahmadi. The island is the third of three loading facilities at the port, each built to accommodate the increased size of oil tankers. Able to serve 375,000-ton tankers, the island lies 10 miles offshore in waters 95 feet deep. Pedestrian bridges secured to the seafloor connect the platforms around the island to one another.

As a member of OPEC, Kuwait must follow guidelines that limit how much oil it may produce and what prices it may set. The sharp drop in oil prices in the 1980s greatly reduced Kuwait's earnings and slowed the nation's efforts to build up other industries. From a high of $34 per barrel in 1981, the price of crude oil reached a low of under $10 per barrel in 1986. OPEC succeeded in raising the price to $18 by early 1987.

In the 1970s and 1980s Kuwait reduced its dependence on the sale of crude oil by developing a market for its refined oil products. Kuwait is also the first OPEC member to explore for oil outside its own borders. Experimental drilling is being conducted in Oman, Angola, Sudan, Congo, Tanzania, and Turkey as well as in the North Sea and the China Sea.

Manufacturing

Using profits from oil, Kuwaiti leaders have encouraged industrialization within the country. The government provides capital, trains workers, and conducts technical studies to help industries get started. The state also provides industries with loans at low interest rates, offers tax breaks, and pays part of the cost of electricity and water.

Courtesy of Embassy of Kuwait

A division of the Petrochemical Industries Company in Shuaiba creates ammonia – a compound of nitrogen and hydrogen used in medicine, explosives, and fertilizers – from petroleum by-products.

With the rise of the oil industry, this limestone brick factory has helped Kuwait meet its rapidly expanding construction needs.

Although these manufacturing efforts have been successful, they cannot compare to the vast wealth that oil wells produce. The growth of industry is hampered by Kuwait's lack of raw materials other than petroleum, a small demand within Kuwait for manufactured items, and a shortage of workers.

Because the oil industry requires only a small percentage of the labor force, the government has allocated sizable funds to provide employment in other parts of the

The Kuwait Flour Mills Company in Shuwaikh produces much of the nation's bread, biscuits, and flour.

The chemical fertilizers manufactured at this plant are essential for agricultural purposes in the desert soil of Kuwait.

economy. For example, in addition to developing positions in petroleum processing, the government created jobs in agriculture, fishing, social welfare, transportation and communications, energy, tourism, and defense. Modern factories in Kuwait produce cement, batteries, electric cables, plastic tubes, woolen blankets, paints, liquid gas, and lime bricks. Most of these manufacturing plants are small.

Imports and exports come and go 24 hours a day at the busy docks in Kuwait's ports.

The government has developed an industrial area at Shuaiba, between Al-Kuwait and Al-Ahmadi. A harbor with a ship repair yard, a fertilizer plant, a water desalinization plant, a seafood packing facility, a cement factory, and a petrochemical complex have all been installed, along with housing for workers and their families.

Imports and Exports

Most of Kuwait's oil is shipped to Japan, the Netherlands, Italy, and Singapore. Exports in the mid-1980s totaled about $8 billion annually, but this figure changes dramatically depending on the world market price and the demand for oil. Besides crude and refined petroleum, Kuwait exports very little. The port of Al-Kuwait traditionally served as a trade and shipping center for pearls and other goods, but the growth of oil production has caused a decline in these industries. Pearl fishing continues on a reduced scale.

Imports come from Japan, the United States, and West Germany. Kuwait spends only about $3.5 billion annually on imports, which gives it a very favorable balance of trade (the difference between money earned from exports and money spent on imports). Major imports include machinery, manufactured goods, food,

57

Agricultural workers pick strawberries in a Kuwaiti greenhouse.

Through the development of greenhouses and the careful cultivation of the land, Kuwaitis are now able to grow a variety of fresh vegetables.

Although pearling is no longer a major economic activity in Kuwait, the industry continues on a small scale. A diver *(right)* prepares for a descent to gather oysters, from which pearls are extracted *(lower left)*. Various implements *(lower right)* are used to sift and measure the pearls.

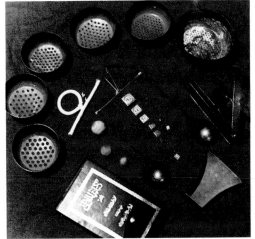

chemicals, and raw materials except for fuels. Kuwait buys most of its military equipment from the Soviet Union.

Agriculture and Fishing

Because of Kuwait's intense heat and vast desert, only 3 percent of its land is considered suitable for farming. The Kuwaiti government has sought to increase agricultural output by irrigating the desert and by starting an experimental farm that produces eggs and milk and that raises poultry. This farm also carries on research in hydroponic farming—a method of growing crops in greenhouses without using soil. Kuwait's principal crops are melons, tomatoes, dates, and onions. The nation still must import much of its food, although its dependence on foreign sources is decreasing.

One of Kuwait's oldest economic activities is fishing. The Persian Gulf has a plentiful supply of fish, and large shrimp are frozen and exported to Europe and the United States. Boat building and a seafood packing plant at Shuaiba add to the fishing industry's facilities. Pearl fishing for the pink pearls off the country's coast is a source of income for some Kuwaitis, and others fashion the pearls into jewelry.

59

The Kuwaiti government has devoted substantial funds to improving the nation's transportation network.

Courtesy of Kuwait Ministry of Information, Safat

Transportation and Communications

Kuwait has a network of more than 2,000 miles of roads, enabling most residents, who generally have their own automobiles, to travel within the country easily. One out of four people in Kuwait owns a car, which exemplifies the nation's high standard of living. Three international highways link Kuwait to Iraq in the north and to Saudi Arabia in the west and south.

The government has discussed plans to connect Al-Kuwait to its surrounding suburbs by rail in order to decrease heavy traffic jams in the capital city. Kuwait International Airport has expanded its facilities to handle increases in the number of passengers and flights. Government-owned Kuwait Airways operates regional and international flights.

The government press, which is equipped with modern printing facilities, publishes

Kuwaitis can find up-to-date information in a wide variety of Arabic and English publications.

Independent Picture Service

With the versatility of the satellite communication system that was established in 1969, Kuwait has improved its contacts with the rest of the world.

books, periodicals, directories, pamphlets, laws, and decrees. Several daily newspapers are published in English, in addition to those printed in Arabic. Various organizations produce a wide range of private magazines, and most publications are circulated to readers free of charge.

The Ministry of Guidance and Information, which spreads news and information, publishes an assortment of magazines, the foremost being *Al-Arabi*. In addition to Kuwait's publications, daily newspapers arrive from abroad by air each morning. Although the press in Kuwait is less restricted than in other Arab countries, the government's fears of political unrest among the Palestinian and Shiite communities have led to increased censorship in the 1980s.

Communications include a telephone network—which is operated as a free public service—and modern telecommunications facilities that connect Kuwait with the rest of the world. Kuwait's first local radio broadcasting station, which was opened in 1951, was very small. It grew during the country's rapid expansion in the 1960s and the 1970s and can now be heard in the United States. Television arrived in Kuwaiti homes in 1961. The Ministry of Guidance and Information supervises radio and television broadcasting.

Modeled after Disneyland in the United States, Entertainment City contains recreational facilities and educational exhibits that have made it one of the biggest attractions in Kuwait.

Tourism

Tourism has not been widely developed in Kuwait, mainly because of the country's lack of attractions for tourists. Nevertheless, Kuwait serves as a connection point for people traveling from eastern Asia to Europe. Most visitors to Kuwait are businesspeople or consultants for the oil industry. Gradually, however, developers are planning entertainment facilities and museums to attract vacationers, and Kuwait may become a destination for more travelers.

Recreational activities include water sports, performances by internationally acclaimed artists, and other entertainment offerings. The Touristic Enterprises Company—92 percent of which is government owned—manages several tourist undertakings, especially on Failaka Island. Two zoological gardens also exist. Entertainment City, modeled after Disneyland in the United States, is located about 12 miles from Al-Kuwait and is a very popular attraction.

The Future

Because Kuwait is a small country surrounded by powerful neighbors, much of the nation's future depends upon the outcome of regional conflicts. With the acceptance of a cease-fire proposal between Iran and Iraq in mid-1988, Kuwait may be able to continue shipping without protection from the U.S. Navy.

Within its own borders, Kuwait is striving to maintain a balance among groups that are often in opposition to the government—Shiites, Sunni fundamentalists, and Palestinians. The nation's vast oil wealth has enabled it to satisfy many of the needs of these groups, but they will probably remain discontent until the Sabah family grants them a more direct political voice. Kuwait is seeking to weaken the influence of its non-Kuwaiti residents by increasing its proportion of Kuwaiti citizens to 50 percent by the year 2000. Thus, although oil has ensured a comfortable standard of living for Kuwaitis, the nation's political future remains uncertain.

Lit up in celebration of the nation's twenty-fifth anniversary of independence in 1986, Kuwait Towers rise prominently in the night sky and symbolize the quick progress Kuwaitis have made since the mid-twentieth century. The towers serve both practical and pleasurable functions—the spheres store water as well as contain an observation booth and a revolving restaurant.

Photo by John Grooters/Reformed Church in America

Index

...